In My Tum

Level 3 – Yellow

Helpful Hints for Reading at Home

The graphemes (written letters) and phonemes (units of sound) used throughout this series are aligned with Letters and Sounds. This offers a consistent approach to learning whether reading at home or in the classroom.

HERE IS A LIST OF PHONEMES FOR THIS PHASE OF LEARNING. AN EXAMPLE OF THE PRONUNCIATION CAN BE FOUND IN BRACKETS.

Phase 3			
j (jug)	v (van)	w (wet)	x (fox)
y (yellow)	z (zoo)	zz (buzz)	qu (quick)
ch (chip)	sh (shop)	th (thin/then)	ng (ring)
ai (rain)	ee (feet)	igh (night)	oa (boat)
oo (boot/look)	ar (farm)	or (for)	ur (hurt)
ow (cow)	oi (coin)	ear (dear)	air (fair)
ure (sure)	er (corner)		

HERE ARE SOME WORDS WHICH YOUR CHILD MAY FIND TRICKY.

Phase 3 Tricky Words			
he	you	she	they
we	all	me	are
be	my	was	her

TOP TIPS FOR HELPING YOUR CHILD TO READ:

• Allow children time to break down unfamiliar words into units of sound and then encourage children to string these sounds together to create the word.

• Encourage your child to point out any focus phonics when they are used.

• Read through the book more than once to grow confidence.

• Ask simple questions about the text to assess understanding.

• Encourage children to use illustrations as prompts.

This book focuses on the phonemes /ch/ and /sh/ and is a yellow level 3 book band.

Can you say this sound and draw it with your finger?

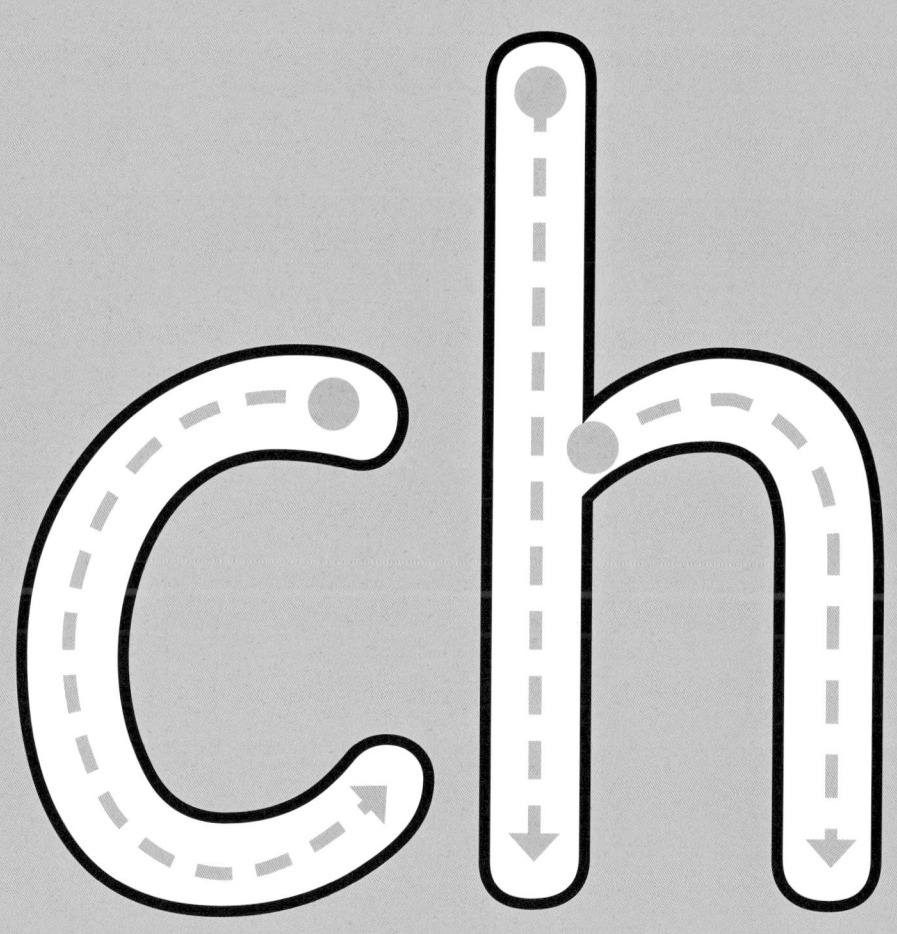

Chop, chop. Mum and Dad chop to fill my tum.

I can dip chips to go in my tum.

Choc-chips are good in my tum.
Yum, yum.

Mash can be fun. Fun mash in my tum.

It will be a salad. A salad in my tum.

Roll roll roll. It will go in my tum.

She fills up her tum. Yum yum yum!

Yum and fun. It is yum in my tum.

©2022 BookLife Publishing Ltd.
King's Lynn, Norfolk PE30 4LS

ISBN 978-1-80155-098-7

All rights reserved. Printed in Poland.
A catalogue record for this book is available from the British Library.

In My Tum
Written by Robin Twiddy
Designed by Gareth Liddington

An Introduction to BookLife Readers...

Our Readers have been specifically created in line with the London Institute of Education's approach to book banding and are phonetically decodable and ordered to support each phase of Letters and Sounds.

Each book has been created to provide the best possible reading and learning experience. Our aim is to share our love of books with children, providing both emerging readers and prolific page-turners with beautiful books that are guaranteed to provoke interest and learning, regardless of ability.

BOOK BAND GRADED using the Institute of Education's approach to levelling.

PHONETICALLY DECODABLE supporting each phase of Letters and Sounds.

EXERCISES AND QUESTIONS to offer reinforcement and to ascertain comprehension.

CLEAR DESIGN to inspire and provoke engagement, providing the reader with clear visual representations of each non-fiction topic.

AUTHOR INSIGHT:
ROBIN TWIDDY

Robin Twiddy is one of BookLife Publishing's most creative and prolific editorial talents, who imbues all his copy with a sense of adventure and energy. Robin's Cambridge-based first class honours degree in psychosocial studies offers a unique viewpoint on factual information and allows him to relay information in a manner that readers of any age are guaranteed to retain. He also holds a certificate in Teaching in the Lifelong Sector, and a post graduate certificate in Consumer Psychology.

A father of two, Robin has written over 70 titles for BookLife and specialises in conceptual, role-playing narratives which promote interaction with the reader and inspire even the most reluctant of readers to fully engage with his books.

This book focuses on the phonemes /ch/ and /sh/ and is a yellow level 3 book band.

Image Credits Images are courtesy of Shutterstock.com. With thanks to Getty Images, Thinkstock Photo and iStockphoto.
Cover – 4–5 –Warut Chinsai, Sergey Novikov. 6–7 – Natalia Lebedinskaia, Krysja. 8–9 – Liderina, AnnGaysorn. 10–11 – DenisProduction.com, 2xSamara.com.

BookLife Non-Fiction Readers

EXPLORE A WORLD OF NON-FICTION WITH OUR DECODABLE READER RANGE

9781839278938

9781839278921

9781839278945

9781839278952

9781839278976

9781839278969

9781839278990

9781839278983

9781839279010

9781839279003

9781839279027

9781839279034

9781839279058

9781839279041

MORE COMING SOON

BookLife Readers

The BookLife Readers begin with the very basics of **phonetically decodable reading**. Starting with the earliest step of **CVC** words – words comprising a consonant, a vowel and a consonant – and building on this combination slowly, the reader follows a prescribed format taken directly from the recognised **Letters and Sounds** educational document.

By aligning our books with Letters and Sounds, we offer our readers a consistent approach to learning, whether at home or in the classroom. The illustrations guide the reader, helping to deliver reading progression through the scheme in a **colourful** and **exciting** way. As a reader moves through the book band levels, the page numbers, level of repetition and sentence structure complexity all advance at a rate which **encourages development** without halting enjoyment.

To find out more about this exciting new reading scheme, visit **www.booklife.co.uk**